A Paines Plough and Belgrade Theatre production
in association with tiata fahodzi

Black Love

by Chinonyerem Odimba,
with music by Ben and Max Ringham

 Paines Plough

 Belgrade Theatre Coventry

 tiata fahodzi

 Supported using public funding by ARTS COUNCIL ENGLAND

Black Love

by Chinonyerem Odimba,
with music by Ben and Max Ringham

Cast

ROO	Leah St Luce
ORION	Nathan Queeley-Dennis
LOIS	Eleanor Sutton
BLACK NOVA (VOICE)	Ayo-Dele Edwards

Production Team

Co-Directors	Chinonyerem Odimba and Katie Posner
Musical Supervisor	Candida Caldicot
Designer	Lydia Denno
Lighting and Video Designer	Gillian Tan
Sound Designer	Kieran Lucas
Movement Director	Kloe Dean
Assistant Director	Kaleya Baxe
Dramaturg	Campbell X
Dramatherapist	Wabriya King
Casting Director	Jacob Sparrow
Costume Supervisor	Rhiannon Hawthorn
Movement Support	Esme Benjamin
Lighting Programmer	Sam Ohlsson
Video Programmer	Ellie Thompson
Company Stage Manager	Aime Neeme
Technical Stage Manager	Benjamin Smith, Philip Thackray
Stage Management Support	Ruth Porter
With thanks to	V&A Productions
	Abbie Morgan

CHINONYEREM ODIMBA (Writer, Co-Director)

Chinonyerem Odimba is a Nigerian British playwright, screenwriter, and poet. Her recent work ranges from MEDEA at Bristol Old Vic, WE TOO, ARE GIANTS for Kiln Theatre, UNKNOWN RIVERS at Hampstead Theatre, PRINCE AND THE PAUPER at Watermill Theatre, THE SEVEN AGES OF PATIENCE at Kiln Theatre, and PRINCESS & THE HUSTLER which toured across the UK for Eclipse Theatre/Bristol Old Vic/Hull Truck. She is also Writer-in-Residence at Royal Welsh College of Music and Drama. Her work for theatre includes THE BIRD WOMAN OF LEWISHAM at the Arcola; RAINY SEASON, and HIS NAME IS ISHMAEL for Bristol Old Vic; JOANNE for Clean Break, and AMONGST THE REEDS for Clean Break/The Yard Theatre. Her work for young people includes a modern retelling of TWIST for Theatre Centre and SWEETNESS OF A STING for NT Connections. She has been shortlisted for several awards including the Adrienne Benham and Alfred Fagon awards. In 2015 her unproduced play WILD IS DE WIND was shortlisted to the final ten for the Bruntwood Playwriting Award. She is the winner for the 2018 Sonia Friedman Award (Channel 4 Playwright Bursary) for a new play HOW TO WALK ON THE MOON, and a finalist for the inaugural Women Playwriting Prize 2020 for her play PARADISE STREET. Chinonyerem's TV credits includes SCOTCH BONNET for BBC Three and A BLUES FOR NIA for BBC/Eclipse Theatre, ADULTING for Channel 4, and more recently MY BEST FRIEND MARRIED A WARRIOR for CBBC. For radio, credits include THE LAST FLAG, and EVE as part of THIS IS YOUR COUNTRY, NOW series on BBC Radio 4. As a director, Chinonyerem has worked for Bristol Old Vic, Theatre503 and Bristol Old Vic Theatre School. She will be co-directing her new play BLACK LOVE for Paines Plough, as well an audio drama for Live Theatre/BBC Radio 4 in 2021. In April 2021, Chinonyerem became the new Artistic Director and Chief Executive of tiata fahodzi.

BEN AND MAX RINGHAM (Music)

Recent work includes: (as creators) ANNA at the National Theatre (Best Sound Design Laurence Olivier Award Nomination). THE CURSE OF THE CRACKLES – Shoreditch Town Hall. LOOKING FOR NIGEL – BBC R and D. (as Composers/Sound Designers) BLINDNESS – The Donmar Warehouse, Daryl Roth Theatre NYC, Teatro de los Insurgentes Mexico City, Teenage Dick, BERBERIAN SOUND STUDIO – at The Donmar Warehouse, CYRANO DE BERGERAC (Best Sound Design Laurence Olivier Award Nomination), BETRAYAL, Pinter at the Pinter – The Jamie Lloyd Company, TARTUFFE – at the National Theatre, THE HAYSTACK – at the Hampstead, THE GIRL ON THE TRAIN, DIAL M FOR MURDER – SF Enterainment, STRANGERS ON A TRAIN for the Ambassador Theatre Group, WHEN THE CROWS VISIT, PASS OVER, THE SEVEN AGES OF PATIENCE at The Kiln, MAN IN THE WHITE SUIT – The Wyndham Theatre, GAMES FOR LOVERS – The Vaults.

LEAH ST LUCE (Roo)

Training: Urdang Academy & The Brit School. Stage Credits: Cover Alice/Tom Cat in DICK WHITTINGTON (National Theatre), Little Eva/Shirelle/Ensemble in BEAUTIFUL (UK Tour), Kathy / Ensemble / Cover Judy in 9 TO 5 The Musical (UK & Ireland Tour), Lisa in MAMMA MIA! (Novello Theatre), Ensemble in CINDERELLA (Chris Hallam, Greenwich Theatre), Corrine in COME BACK AND GONE (Claire Grove, BBC Radio 4), Zonia in JOE TURNER'S COME AND GONE (David Lan, The Young Vic), OLIVER! (Cameron Mackintosh), Patty in HANDLE AND SPOUT (Cartoonito Karaoke), Young Nala in DISNEY'S THE LION KING (Lyceum Theatre).

NATHAN QUEELEY-DENNIS (Orion)

Nathan Queeley-Dennis is an Actor & Writer from Birmingham. A former MonologueSlam winner, his theatre credits include LITTLE BABY JESUS (Birmingham Rep), REBEL MUSIC

(Middle Child), A TASTE OF HONEY (National Theatre) and his own written piece BULLRING TECHNO MAKEOUT JAMZ (The Vaults & Bunker Theatre).

ELEANOR SUTTON (Lois)

Eleanor's theatre credits include: THE CRUCIBLE and A LITTLE NIGHT MUSIC (Chester Storyhouse); AMADEUS (National Theatre); FUTURE CONDITIONAL (The Old Vic); THE MASTER BUILDER (The Old Vic); THE WIZARD OF OZ (Leeds Playhouse); WINDOWS (Finborough Theatre) and AS YOU LIKE IT (UK tour).

AYO-DELE EDWARDS (Voice of BLACK NOVA)

Ayo-Dele trained at Mountview Theatre School. She is an actress, singer and songwriter and Podcast Host, she is interested in theatre that: Empowers, inspires and furthers the conversation about our narratives, using multi-disciplinary forms; poetry, music, storytelling, dance, and movement. BECOMING (solo show), a musical drama combining storytelling and original songs to bring to life a story of growing up across two continents, exploring identity, love, fear, family relationships and migration, is her first written play which debuted at Stratford Circus Arts Centre during women's international week. She recently launched a brand new podcast called BECOMING YOU (available on all major digital platforms) where she speaks with men and women about how their creativity helps them deal with life's ups and downs. Short film: WAKE UP (Amazon Prime) STILL BREATHING, Sheldonian Theatre Oxford. HERE'S WHAT SHE SAID TO ME, Utopia Theatre/Sheffield Theatres. Other theatre credits include 5 star nominated, smash hit UK production of THE SECRET LIVES OF BABA SEGI'S WIVES, Elufowoju Jr Ensemble, Arcola Theatre, and Lagos Nigeria Mama Bolanle/Ensemble/ Choral Associate IYALODE OF ETI (DUCHESS OF MALFI) (Utopia Theatre/West Yorkshire Playhouse) on Tour & Ake Festival (Lagos) 2016.

KATIE POSNER (Co-Director)

Katie joined Paines Plough as Joint Artistic Director with Charlotte Bennett in August 2019. She is currently directing the Paines Plough Roundabout 2021 season, which includes HUNGRY by Chris Bush, REALLY BIG AND REALLY LOUD by Phoebe Eclair-Powell and BLACK LOVE by Chinonyerem Odimba, which she is co-directing with Chinonyerem Odimba.

Katie is an experienced and award-winning director. She has worked across a wide variety of productions both overseas and on national tours, including multiple productions with York Theatre Royal and Pilot Theatre with whom she was Associate Director from 2009 until 2017. Her work encompasses both intimate pieces of new writing and larger-scale community pieces. In 2019 Katie received a UK Theatre Award nomination as Best Director with her production of MY MOTHER SAID I NEVER SHOULD at Theatre By The Lake. Recent productions include: MY MOTHER SAID I NEVER SHOULD (Theatre By The Lake), MOLD RIOTS (Theatr Clwyd) and THE SEVEN AGES OF PATIENCE (Kiln Theatre). Recent credits include: SWALLOWS & AMAZONS (Storyhouse), BABE (Mercury Theatre), PLAYING UP (NYT), FINDING NANA (New Perspectives), MADE IN INDIA (Tamasha, Belgrade, Pilot), EVERYTHING IS POSSIBLE: THE YORK SUFFRAGETTES (York Theatre Royal), THE SEASON TICKET (Northern Stage), A VIEW FROM ISLINGTON NORTH (Out Of Joint), IN FOG AND FALLING SNOW (National Railway Museum), RUNNING ON THE CRACKS (Tron Theatre), END OF DESIRE (York Theatre Royal), YORK MYSTERY PLAYS (Museum Gardens York), BLACKBIRD, GHOST TOWN, CLOCKING IN, A RESTLESS PLACE (Pilot Theatre).

CANDIDA CALDICOT (Musical Supervisor)

Musical Director credits: THE LEHMAN TRILOGY (Broadway, West End, National Theatre); THE WIZARD OF OZ (Leeds Playhouse); KING LEAR (Duke of

York's); THE SEVEN AGES OF PATIENCE (Kiln); CARMEN – THE GYPSY (UK Tour); PETER PAN (Regent's Park Open Air Theatre); THE LITTLE MERMAID (Metta Theatre, UK Tour); THE SHADOW FACTORY (Nuffield); WOYZECK (Old Vic); BEYOND THE FENCE (Sky Arts, Arts Theatre); IT'S A MAD WORLD MY MASTERS (ETT); QUEEN ANNE; HECUBA; THE WITCH OF EDMONTON; THE HERESY OF LOVE; THE HEART OF ROBIN HOOD (RSC); THE TEMPEST (RSC, US Tour); LOVE'S LABOURS LOST (Oxford Shakespeare Company); GALILEO (Birmingham Rep). As Composer: ZERAFFA GIRAFFA (Little Angel & Omnibus); Buckets (Orange Tree); 4 PEPYS (Wilderness Festival); HANSEL AND GRETEL; TREASURE ISLAND; MUCH ADO ABOUT NOTHING; PINOCCHIO; RICHARD III; ALICE IN WONDERLAND; ALICE THROUGH THE LOOKING GLASS; ROMEO AND JULIET; WIND IN THE WILLOWS (Iris Theatre); Macbeth (Shakespeare in Styria); ONCE UPON A TIME (Booktrust Tour); THE HOSTAGE (Southwark Playhouse). Candida is the composer of THE LITTLE PRINCE THE MUSICAL which has released an EP and is now in development. She was also Musical Director on two new musicals for NYMT: PRODIGY and THE BATTLE OF BOAT both of which have released original cast albums.

LYDIA DENNO (Designer)

Lydia is a visual artist. She studied Theatre Design at Nottingham Trent and graduated in 2007. She began her career as assistant designer on the award-winning Railway Children (National Railway Museum and King's Cross Theatre), and has gone on to develop an interdisciplinary practice which encompasses theatre, installation, illustration and even walking. She has worked for theatres such as York Theatre Royal, Nottingham Playhouse, The Lowry, Soho Theatre and Wembley Arena, as well as heritage sites around the UK and galleries internationally. Lydia's design work has been awarded an Eastern Eye Award and recently 'gained laurels' having been selected for the

Tribeca Film Festival. She is excited by the stories that spaces and objects can tell, as well as the people that inhabit and use them. With Iraqi-British heritage, she is interested in cross-cultural storytelling and in particular stories that transcend physical and metaphysical borders. She is drawn towards under-represented stories and characters, interested in fleeting moments and gestures as performance, and enticed by what narratives lie in the detail.

GILLIAN TAN (Lighting and Video Designer)

Gillian is a multi-disciplinary designer, working across lighting and video for various theatrical, immersive and interactive experiences. Theatre credits include: SOUTH PACIFIC (Chichester Festival Theatre), ALYSSA, MEMOIRS OF A QUEEN (Vaudeville Theatre), AISHA AND ABHAYA (Royal Ballet/Rambert); MAJESTIQUE (Skråen); THE SONG PROJECT – IS IN OUR BLOOD (Royal Court Theatre); 4.48 PSYCHOSIS (revival. Lyric Hammersmith/Royal Opera House); LA SOIRÉE (Aldwych Theatre/Southbank Centre/Skråen); CORALINE (Barbican Theatre/Royal Opera House); TAMBURLAINE (Arcola Theatre); INVISIBLE TREASURE (Ovalhouse Theatre); WHO DO WE THINK WE ARE (Southwark Playhouse); CROCODILES (Royal Exchange, Manchester). Film credits: NYX AND GAZELLE TWIN PRESENT: DEEP ENGLAND, a performance film by Iain Forsyth and Jane Pollard, HELD MOMENTARILY (RAM). She is also a member of the Somerset House Exchange and is the Head of Video at RADA.

KIERAN LUCAS (Sound Designer)

Kieran is an award-nominated sound designer & theatre-maker. He is a founding member of Barrel Organ & associate artist at Coney. Credits include: THE FUTURE PROJECT (Streatham Space Project), FOUND SOUND (Coventry Creates/Coventry City of Culture), NOAH & THE PEACOCK (Nottingham Playhouse), ME FOR THE

WORLD (Young Vic), THE RAGE OF NARCISSUS (Pleasance Islington), ANTIGONE (New Diorama), GASTRONOMIC (Shoreditch Town Hall/Norwich Theatre Royal), CONSPIRACY (Underbelly/New Diorama), POPS (HighTide Festival) COMPANION: MOON (Natural History Museum), HOW WE SAVE THE WORLD (Natural History Museum), THE EX-BOYFRIEND YARD SALE (CPT/Progress Festival), TBCTV (Somerset House), SQUARE GO (Paines Plough Roundabout/59E59), A GIRL IN SCHOOL UNIFORM (Walks Into A Bar) (New Diorama), MY NAME IS RACHEL CORRIE (Young Vic), BIG GUNS (The Yard), UNDER THE SKIN (St Paul's Cathedral).

KLOE DEAN (Movement Director)

Kloe is a Choreographer, Movement Director and Performing Artist from London, UK, specialising in hip-hop, funk and streetdance styles. Kloe is a Work Place artist at The Place, Kings Cross, Creative Director of all-female hip-hop dance company, Myself UK Dance, and has presented a range of dance theatre both nationally and internationally including Breakin Convention in London, Ladies Of Hip Hop in New York and The Sub Urban Danse Festival Copenhagen. Kloé has worked with a range of music artists including Little Simz, Cleo Sol and Rita Ora, as well as brands such as Jimmy Choo, Nike, Marks & Spencer's and George at ASDA.

KALEYA BAXE (Assistant Director)

Kaleya Baxe is a writer, director and facilitator whose work is driven by her passion for representation, inclusion and a collaborative process. As well as working on outreach and youth projects with the Young Vic, Kiln, Arcola Theatre and several drama schools, her work often shines a light on important subjects (PATRICIA GETS READY (FOR A DATE WITH THE MAN THAT USED TO HIT HER) and has toured schools, youth settings and pupil referral units (WRITTEN, Little Fish Theatre). As an assistant she has

worked with acclaimed writers such as Chinonyerem Odimba (Artistic Director, Tiata Fahodzi) and Mike Bartlett (Doctor Foster, Life). Kaleya trained at the Royal Central School of Speech and Drama on the Drama, Applied Theatre and Education course. Her work as a director includes; 786 by Ric Renton (Paines Plough R&D, LAMDA), PATRICIA GETS READY (FOR A DATE WITH THE MAN THAT USED TO HIT HER) by Martha Watson Allpress (Pleasance, VAULT Festival Show of the Week Award Winner) and WRITTEN by Alex Cooke (Little Fish Theatre, Schools and Youth Settings Tour).

CAMPBELL X (Dramaturg)

Campbell X is a writer/director who directed the award-winning queer urban romantic comedy feature film STUD LIFE. His film STUD LIFE was voted by the Guardian as one of the top 10 Black British feature films ever made. It was also in Vogue magazine as one of the best films to watch in 2020. STUD LIFE was also selected by the British Film Institute as one of the top 8 queer films to view while we were all on lockdown. Campbell was one of the writers at the Royal Court for MY WHITE BEST FRIEND theatre series. Campbell directed and produced the short film DES!RE, the documentary VISIBLE which headlined the Scottish Queer Film Festival in December 2018. Campbell directed the award-winning TV webseries DIFFERENT FOR GIRLS and is one of the directors of the transgender webseries SPECTRUM LONDON. Campbell's recent film STILL WE THRIVE is about Black joy and resistance. Campbell is the co-founder with Neelu Bhuman of Wahala Film Fund https://www.wahalafilmfund.com a completion fund for short films by and about QTIPOC people.

WABRIYA KING (Dramatherapist)

Wabriya graduated as an actress from The Oxford School of Drama in 2012. After several years working as an actress in a variety of roles, she decided to take her career in a different direction and graduated from the University of Roehampton with an MA in Dramatherapy in 2019. Since qualifying, she has worked alongside: ROMEO & JULIET – Shakespeare's Globe, THE DEATH OF A BLACK MAN- Hampstead Theatre, SEVEN METHODS OF KILLING KYLIE JENNER – The Royal Court, SHUCK N JIVE – Soho Theatre, 846 Live -Theatre Royal Stratford East, TYPICAL – Soho Theatre, THE HIGH TABLE – Bush Theatre. She believes that the arts have a responsibility to its performers to support their mental health wellbeing. This is clearly a shared belief as her work is gaining momentum within the sector.

tour and a large background in fringe theatre and outdoor events. Phil currently works as freelance theatre and live event technician having worked often with Theatr Clywd on a number of their productions and with T-bats for their outdoor events. Credits-Technical Crew ROUNDABOUT TOUR – 2019. Senior Build Crew and Senior Event Supervisor GUNG HO tour 2018, 2019. Stage Technician 2018 HANSEL & GRETEL: FAIRYTALE DETECTIVES -Theatr Clywd.

AIME NEEME (Company Stage Manager)

Aime is a LAMDA trained freelance theatre director and stage manager. Past credits include; PARAKEET (Boundless), HARD FEELINGS, THE HOTEL PLAYS, A LIE OF THE MIND (Defibrillator Theatre), DENNIS OF PENGE (Ovalhouse).

BENJAMIN SMITH (Technical Stage Manager)

Benjamin graduated from the Stage Management and Technical Theatre course at the Royal Welsh College of Music and Drama in 2018. Since leaving he has had a varied work career, Sound Designing, Re-Lighting, as well as both Technical and Company Stage Management. Previous work includes: JANE EYRE (Blackeyed Theatre), ANIMAL FARM (Pegasus Theatre), ANNA KARENINA (Pegasus Theatre), UNFORTUNATE (Fat Rascal Theatre), VULVARINE (Fat Rascal Theatre), WORD GET'S AROUND (RCT Theatre), MEMORY OF WATER (ALRA North), 2023 (Illumine Theatre Company).

PHILIP THACKRAY (Technical Stage Manager)

Philip Thackray is one of this technical stage managers for this year's Roundabout tour, having worked previously on the 2019 Roundabout

Paines Plough

Paines Plough are a touring theatre company dedicated to new writing; we find, develop and empower writers across the country and share their explosive new stories with audiences all over the UK and beyond.

'The lifeblood of the UK's theatre ecosystem.' *Guardian*

Since 1974 Paines Plough has worked with over 300 outstanding British playwrights including James Graham, Sarah Kane, Dennis Kelly, Mike Bartlett, Sam Steiner, Elinor Cook, Vinay Patel, Zia Ahmed and Kae Tempest.

Our plays are nationally identified and locally heard. We tour to over 40 places a year and are committed to bringing work to communities who might not otherwise have the opportunity to experience much new writing or theatre. We reach over 30,000 people annually from Cornwall to the Orkney Islands, in village halls and in our own pop-up theatre Roundabout; a state of the art, in the round auditorium which travels the length and breadth of the country.

'That noble company Paines Plough, de facto national theatre of new writing.' *Daily Telegraph*

Furthering our reach beyond theatre walls our audio app COME TO WHERE I'M FROM hosts 180 original mini plays about home and our digital projects connect with audiences via WhatsApp, phone, email and even by post.

Wherever you are, you can experience a Paines Plough Production.

'I think some theatre just saved my life.' @kate_clement on Twitter

Paines Plough Limited is a company limited by guarantee and a registered charity.
Registered Company no: 1165130
Registered Charity no: 267523

Paines Plough, 2nd Floor, 10 Leake Street, London SE1 7NN
+ 44 (0) 20 7240 4533

office@painesplough.com
www.painesplough.com

Follow @PainesPlough on Twitter
Follow @painesplough on Instagram
Like Paines Plough at facebook.com/PainesPloughHQ
Donate to Paines Plough at justgiving.com/PainesPlough

ROUNDABOUT

'A beautifully designed masterpiece in engineering' *The Stage*

ROUNDABOUT is Paines Plough's beautiful portable in-the-round theatre. It's a completely self-contained 168-seat auditorium that flat packs into a single lorry and pops up anywhere from theatres to school halls, sports centres, warehouses, car parks and fields.

We built ROUNDABOUT to tour to places that don't have theatres. ROUNDABOUT travels the length and breadth of the UK bringing the nation's best playwrights and a thrilling theatrical experience to audiences everywhere.

Over the last six years ROUNDABOUT has hosted over 2,000 hours of entertainment for more than 100,000 people in places ranging from a churchyard in Salford to Margate seafront.

ROUNDABOUT was designed by Lucy Osborne and Emma Chapman at Studio Three Sixty in collaboration with Charcoalblue and Howard Eaton.

WINNER of Theatre Building of the Year at The Stage Awards 2014

'ROUNDABOUT venue wins most beautiful interior venue by far @edfringe.'

@ChaoticKirsty on Twitter

'ROUNDABOUT is a beautiful, magical space. Hidden tech make it Turkish-bath-tranquil but with circus-tent-cheek. Aces.'

@evenicol on Twitter

ROUNDABOUT was made possible thanks to the belief and generous support of the following Trusts and individuals and all who named a seat in Roundabout. We thank them all.

TRUSTS AND FOUNDATIONS
Andrew Lloyd Webber Foundation
Paul Hamlyn Foundation
Garfield Weston Foundation
J Paul Getty Jnr Charitable Trust
John Ellerman Foundation

CORPORATE
Universal Consolidated Group
Howard Eaton Lighting Ltd
Charcoalblue
Avolites Ltd
Factory Settings
Total Solutions

Roundabout is supported by the Theatres Trust in 2021.

Theatres
Trust

Pop your name on a seat and help us pop-up around the UK:
www.justgiving.com/fundraising/roundaboutauditorium

Paines Plough

Supported using public funding by
ARTS COUNCIL ENGLAND

Belgrade
Theatre
Coventry

Together, with the diverse communities across Coventry and the region, we aim to enrich and fundamentally change people's lives for the better through theatre.

In our landmark building, across the region, the UK and online, we will use theatre to entertain, inspire, share the city's stories, uncover hidden histories and unleash the creativity in our communities.

The Belgrade is the largest professional theatre in Coventry and so we act as both the city and region's commercial and producing theatre. We are also highly respected for our ground-breaking community and education initiatives. Hamish Glen is the current Artistic Director and Chief Executive.

The Belgrade is a registered charity and receives revenue funding from Coventry City Council and Arts Council England as well as project funding from these and other government sources.

The Belgrade played a key role in securing Coventry as UK City of Culture 2021 and in 2019 we appointed Corey Campbell, Balisha Karra and Justine Themen as Co-Artistic Directors, with a remit to programme and direct the Theatre's produced work for UK City of Culture 2021.

Senior Management Team:

Hamish Glen
CHIEF EXECUTIVE & ARTISTIC DIRECTOR

Joanna Reid
EXECUTIVE DIRECTOR

Corey Campbell
2021 CO-ARTISTIC DIRECTOR

Balisha Karra
2021 CO-ARTISTIC DIRECTOR

Justine Themen
2021 CO-ARTISTIC DIRECTOR

Sâmir Bhamra
2021 SENIOR PRODUCER

Vera Ding
GENERAL MANAGER

Adrian Sweeney
DIRECTOR OF PRODUCTION

Richard Hope-Jones
GENERAL MANAGER – BPS

Nicola Young
DIRECTOR OF COMMUNICATIONS

Ray Clenshaw
COMMUNICATIONS MANAGER

Helen Hotchkiss
HEAD OF DEVELOPMENT

Paul Newsome
FINANCIAL CONTROLLER

Founded in 1997, tiata fahodzi is the UK's leading British African heritage theatre company and is led by Artistic Director Chinonyerem Odimba.

tiata fahodzi makes theatre that looks around and looks forward, with a mission to tell contemporary stories in surprising and innovative ways. We aim to celebrate and champion artists and creatives with an experience of what it is to be of African heritage in the Britain of today. We believe that it is possible to see ourselves in our full complexity and joy.

At tiata fahodzi, we make social change the sole driving force behind what we do. When we use the word community, we don't mean the things happening outside of our buildings and theatre institutions, but instead we recognise we are part of a much bigger community, and that it is possible for all of us to be creatives, make work, enjoy culture, and fight for the arts.

The company is at an exciting point in its history as it heads into its 25th anniversary, we hope we can build on and shine a light on the ways in which it has contributed so much already to the British theatre landscape.

tiata fahdozi is an engine room for so many of the conversations that artists, audiences and communities from a British African heritage want to have. We want to see an Arts and Cultural ecology in Britain where everyone feels invited and welcome to participate, and a theatre industry that is a more dynamic and inclusive place for everyone.

Black Love is the company's first musical and is written and co-directed by Chinonyerem Odimba , who says of the play:

Black Love is really what it says. It is the expression of love that exists in families, siblings, friends, lovers and more. The idea of Black Love really lies in wanting audiences to see the kind of relationship that is everyday for some, and somehow invisible to others. The family in the story, and the extent of love that exists between them was wonderful to create.

This play is about the ways in which that love is interrupted/disrupted, and the defiance of knowing that that love should be given the space and time to fully exist and be seen.

Previous work by tiata fahodzi includes *seeds* by Melanie Pennant, *good dog* by Arinzé Kene, *mixed brain* by ITV *Benidorm*'s Nathan Bryon, *bricks and pieces* by award-winning Charlene James, *i know all the secrets in my world* by Natalie Ibu, and the Olivier-nominated production *iya ile (the first wife)* by Oladipo Agboluaje, and *the gods are not to blame* by Bola Agbaje.

Contact tiata fahodzi – info@tiatfahodzi.com

tiata fahodzi is an Arts Council England National Portfolio Organisation.

BLACK LOVE

Book and lyrics by Chinonyerem Odimba

Music by Ben and Max Ringham

Black Love is the day my mother opened her Black legs and let
my Black father come inside her Black-framed sacredness…
Black Love is my name.
Black Love is the look from my Black grandmother that burned
itself through skin, soul and spirit.
Black Love is that red dust I remember inhaling.
Black Love is my mouth wide open waiting to be fed by Black
breasts.
Black Love is watching my brothers and my sister be born from
that same Black place.
Black Love is the sun on my face in a place where my
Blackness is not a question.
Black Love is every day I look in the mirror and accept myself
inch by inch.
Black Love is my daughter's name.
Black Love is everything I can do to not believe in your version
of me.

Chinonyerem Odimba, 2020

- **Black Love has to be unrelenting resilient in order to
withstand any pitfalls that other relationship, without the
need to survive, might succumb to in falling apart.**

- **Is finding the person who sees and loves me no matter
what.**

- **Feels right. Less explaining. Less explaining away.**

Characters

BLACK NOVA – *a person sometimes – a soundscape sometimes*

ROO – *twenty-two-year-old Black British woman. Roo lives with her brother. Roo has lived in London all her life. She works as a youth support worker. She's a big fan of music festivals. She is also part of a local choir*

ORION – *twenty-five-year-old Black British man. Orion has lived abroad in the past but now lives in London with his sister. He is an actor*

LOIS – *twenty-four-year-old White British/European woman. Lois has hair scraped back in a high ponytail, with her baby hair gelled down at the front. She wears large hooped earrings and is obsessed with her false, long, well-kept nails. Lois has lived in London all her life. She is a big fan of grime and Afrobeat music, and always goes to Notting Hill Carnival*

Settings

HOME – *Roo and Orion's small flat.*

OUT – *Anywhere that is not home.*

Notes

All text in **bold** is verbatim speech – no changes can be made to this text. These lines are random voices in the style of vox pops.

Text in *italics* aligned to the left is sung.

Text in *italics* aligned to right is an aside, addressed directly to the audience.

Words in *italics* indicate emphasis.

An ellipsis (…) indicates a trailing-off or pause at the end of dialogue.

A forward slash (/) indicates an overlap in speech.

This text went to press before the end of rehearsals and so may differ slightly from the play as performed.

PART ONE

1.

CAST.
Black Love

BLACK NOVA.
Black Love is the day my mother opened her Black legs and let my Black father come inside her Black-framed sacredness…

CAST.
Black Love

BLACK NOVA.
Is my name

CAST.
Black Love

BLACK NOVA.
Is the look from my Black grandmother that burned itself through skin, soul and spirit

CAST.
Black Love

BLACK NOVA.
Is that red dust I remember inhaling

CAST.
Black Love

BLACK NOVA.
Is my mouth wide open waiting to be fed by Black breasts

And it hits their ears like molten fire
Burns you know
Comes faster than lava

It's not what they want to hear
So the chase begins again

CAST.
  Black Love

BLACK NOVA.
  Is watching my brothers and my sister be born from that
  same Black place

CAST.
  Black Love

BLACK NOVA.
  Is the sun on my face in a place where my Blackness is not a
  question

CAST.
  Black Love

BLACK NOVA.
  Black Love is every day I look in the mirror and accept
  myself

CAST.
  Black Love

BLACK NOVA.
  Is my daughter's name
  Black Love is everything I can do to not believe in your
  version of me

  Black Love is / Black Love is / Black Love is / Black Love is /
  Black Love is / Black Love is / Black Love is / Black Love is /
  Black Love is / Black Love is /

  BLACK NOVA *enters, running.*

BLACK NOVA. Whew.
  Chile.
  This game.
  This race.
  What a time.

  Stops. Looks up – bends down and starts panting.

We are running again.
Creating havoc again.
Playing chase and catch-up again.

And what a time!

Stands up –

And this is the game you see.
They say –

'You better start speaking up!
You better tell us the truth.
We can't let you go until you do.'

Laughs –

It's not what they want to hear…

And it hits their ears like molten fire – burns you know –
comes faster than lava.

So the chase, the game begins again.

Laughs again –

So you will see me run again and again.
Never knowing if next time they catch me, they will ask
again –

'What is your truth?
In your words…'

Beat.

My friends…

You are my friends aren't you?

My friends…

Something happened long ago…
And now I am here.
My existence is unknown.
Unfounded.
Things colliding.
I am a result of all of those things colliding…

It's not what they want to hear.

So the chase, the game begins again.

BLACK NOVA *runs one way – then another way – then exits.*

2. Home

ROO *stands alone.*
Candles lit.
A bunch of peonies sit prominently.
She glances across the faces staring back at her.
She is watching them as much as they are watching her.

ROO. Yoni.
 Hoohoo.
 Punani.
 Lady V.
 Alter of love.
 Lady garden.
 Pussy.
 Vajayjay.
 Vaginaland.
 Woo-woo.
 Love tunnel.

Whatever you want to call it.
We're here to talk about it.
For those who don't know my name is Aurora… Roo to you!

This is a space for you to heal from the centuries of
patriarchal mess that society has created around our bodies.
Tonight we will be honouring the most sacred and softest
parts of us.
Our. Pussyhole. Will. Be. Our. Temple /

ORION *enters.*
He is muttering –

ORION. I'm just a simple guy…
That's all I am…
I'm a simple good guy who's fallen in love. That's all I am.

Beat.

Yo! I'm sorry I…
You alright everyone…

ORION *waves an awkward greeting to the audience.*

ROO. Or!

ORION. I'm gone you know.

ORION *exits.*

Beat.

Song: 'Pussyhole'

ROO.
It's my pussy so I'll do what I like
Like a universe waiting to be explored
Just waiting to be licked open
To be adored
Just to be adored

3. Home

ORION *is sitting in front of a camera set up on a tripod.*

ORION. Hello.

> *I should just say hi… better…*

Yes. Hello!

> *What you saying yes to you dickhead?*

My name is Orion Hammond.

> *That's a strong opening.*

I am an actor. I think a good one.

ROO*'s voice breaks into* ORION*'s world – she is not seen.*

Song: 'Pussyhole'

ROO.
Sing it loud!
This is my pussyhole /
This is my pussyhole

What?

ORION *moves his chair closer to the camera –*

ORION. I'm reading for the part of Joe…
I got the script fine…

Obvs.

Couldn't put it down.

Fast enough.

Yes.

If I say yes like that one more time then I think I can slap
myself for real.

ROO.
When I touch it
Magic happens
And when I look at it, it just glows /

ORION.
Like. Wow.

Lies.

So I'm really excited by this!

It's true I kind of am.

My first big break and I'm so grateful you know… that
you've invited me to audition… and I am really just blown
away…

I'm playing that fake humble grateful bullshit. They love it.

ROO.
It's my pussy so I'll do what I like
Like a universe waiting to be explored
Just waiting to be licked open
To be adored
Just to be adored

ORION. *Do you think they're hearing this?*

The script is great. And the writing is just so…
I mean all these characters really feel… alive you know…
jump off the page and I can totally see them.

You're repeating Orion.

And I can totally see myself in this role… I really do think I
share so many of Joe's characteristics… and even the way
he's described as *dashing*…

My Spotlight profile isn't really that up to date but…

ROO.
The juice is real I know
The pleasure unknown
Just give me your finger so
And let's see how long we can go /

ORION. I'm five-ten.

Basically like six foot.

I'm working out every day.

Let me just show them so…

ORION *stands – flexes – and quickly sits back down in
position –*

I can do a variety of accents…
Or just London.
RP.
Or like yardie vibes…

What. Am. I. Talking. About?

Well you know…

Imagine if they had a bloody clue!

ROO.
Like a garden full of the sweetest flowers
A rare orchid
To be adored
Just to be adored…

ORION. Okay I'll just read it now.

In an American accent? You sure bruv?

(*In an American accent.*) I'm just a simple guy. That's all I am. I'm a simple good guy who's fallen in love. That's all I am. I'm not sure if you know how much I love you. If you know how much I want you. Don't go back there. Stay here with me. Stay here and I'll give you everything you could ever need. Everything.

ROO.
Orgasm

ORION. You hear me? You'll be wanting for nothing. Not with me by your side. What you think? Will you? Can you want me too?

ROO.
Orgasm

ORION. Want a simple blockhead like me? Want this simple life I'm offering? Say something goddamn it! Can't you see you're driving me crazy? Can't you see how much I want you?

ROO.
Orgasm

Beat.

ORION. I'll do the next scene I prepared now…

ROO.
Orgasm

Orgasm.

Orgasm

Orgasm.

ORION. For fuck's sake Roo!
  What was that?
  Fuck it!
  Fuck it all!

4. Home

ROO *and* ORION *enter simultaneously* –

ROO. Or!

ORION. Roo for fuck's sake!

ROO. You know it's every Wednesday!

ORION. I forgot /

ROO. If the group think there's a man just listening in /

ORION. Listening in?
  What the hell?
  I was trying to do a thing!

ROO. It really fucks with the energy and space we create for
  ourselves /

ORION. You were shouting 'pussyhole' and 'orgasm' over and
  over.
  What kind of energy is that going to give to my audition?

ROO. You could hear us?

ORION (*mocking*). – My sacred flower.
  This garden of Eden…
  Touch me touch me /

ROO. You're a dick!

  They both burst into laughter –

Seriously though. It's important. Do you know how much damage this world is doing to Black women's relationship to their bodies? Dress one way. You're a hoe. Or too ghetto. Dress another way. You're trying too hard.

God forbid if we actually enjoy sex!

ORION. I get it.

ROO. We have to liberate ourselves from all forms of sexual and spiritual bondage.

ORION. Unless you've bought the handcuffs yourself right?

ROO. Exactly bruv!

ORION. Is there a power salute for the women's regions?

ROO. VAGINA!

ORION. I do get it. Seriously. I do. And I'm well impressed that you doing the training on sexual health and all that.

That's my sis yeah?

ROO *and* ORION *perform a well-rehearsed dance of hand and face gestures –*

ROO. What was the audition for?

ORION. Another supporting role. White woman's house-help-cum-butler… and by cum I mean /

ROO. Oh shit! So she's fucking him as well as telling him how to hold the tray?

ORION. But this is the thing…
It's bullshit.
I just don't know what the fuck I'm meant to do if this is all I'm ever going to get /

ROO. What would Mum do?

ORION. Don't do that.

ROO. True though.

ORION. Relax yeah.

ROO. You're going to have to talk about her some time.
   Like she's why we're like this. Remember?
   That's the promise we made.
   She wasn't ordinary, she was extraordinary and /

ORION. I know! I was there!

   I've got stuff to do /

ROO. Don't run away.

ORION. I'm not /

ROO. You're thinking about it though aren't you?

ORION. No!

ROO. Yes you are!
   I can tell.
   You've been looking at flights… I saw it in your search
   history.
   What am I meant to do if you go /

ORION. Looking at flights doesn't mean I'm disappearing.

ROO. Not really talking about her for nearly a year now does
   though.

   Beat.

   I know everything here reminds you of her.
   Her things…
   I know…
   I remind you of her…

   ROO *moves closer than before –*
   She takes his hand –

   I don't know what to do with this either.
   Like I don't even know what we're meant to say make it
   better.
   Like is this something you're just meant to wake up one
   morning and forget 'bout like that?
   I mean people say all this *stuff* don't they? All this stuff
   about what the right thing to do is… I mean that's the people
   who are still around…

Lost for words.

Look at me blank.

Like there's something on my face they don't want to tell me about. Fuck it!

What is it?

What's on my face bruv?

Then I remember that all I'm doing all day and all night is floating between this place and that other place where all the things that held us together used to happen.

The strands of sinew and tears and jokes that was *us*.

But before we were just playing because we had her.

Now...

Now we have to do the fighting for her.

Fuck the things that try to reduce women like her to just a stereotype /

ORION. Fuck auditions where I'm meant to play Black Man One or Two... I am... I am more than that...

ROO. Fuck not seeing me for the spirit full, life full, 4C-Afro full mess that I am...

ORION. Fuck always playing the badman...

The dodgy mate...

Be the shoplifter...

The village-idiot boyfriend /

ROO. Fuck all the boxes you want to put us in!

ORION. Fuck I'm tired!

Beat.

ROO. I know...

Song: 'Constellations'

ORION.

You are the best sis

The only one

Never going to be without you

Never going to be apart

You make me smile from the morning to the night
Keep my feet right on the ground
And my soul soaring in the sky

Don't know this life without you
Don't know this world without us
And that's just the way that it is…
Brother and sister
Black Love like no other
Take what you will but don't give me another sister

Aurora and Orion
Constellation in time
More than blood
More than just fam

You are the best sis
The only one
Never going to be without you
Never going to be apart…

ORION *and* ROO.
Aurora and Orion
Constellations in time
More than blood
More than just fam

ORION.
You are the best sis
The only one
Never going to be without you
Never going to be apart

Beat.

You won't ever leave Roo will you?

ROO. Go where though!

More than blood
More than just fam

Beat.

ORION. Orgasm!

ROO. You really heard everything…

ORION. Yes I did.

> ORION *places his head on* ROO*'s shoulder. Closes his eyes –*

> Where do you think she is Roo?

ROO. She's somewhere beautiful.
She is…

> A halo.
> A glow.
> Maybe it's paradise.
> All yellow.
> All green.
> Everything soft…
> Velvet softness of a Black butterfly's wing.
> Velvety sunshine.
> Rays.
> Open sky-blues.

5.

BLACK NOVA *enters.*

BLACK NOVA.
I'm still contracting…
In this world,
Our world,
There is a love
Which has no bounds.

> Refuses to live just in the limitations of your mind.
> It is a real magic,
> Working through days and nights,

Long existed before the measures of time.
I'm still contracting...

It invokes generations across lands.
Sitting around dinner tables,
Black mouths laugh at Black family jokes.
Period drama or science fiction,
I'm still contracting...

And in that romantic film...
Let Black lips kiss on Black lips.
And let that Black lust spill
Into our naughtiest fantasies.
I'm still contracting...

Soft hands holding the Black hands of our younger folks,
As they skip down the street.
Towards the same promise,
Of sunshine and beach holidays.
I'm still contracting...

And in this picture of a family mourning,
Stood by an empty hole,
But now it's our Black grandmother
Whose memories we evoke.
I'm still contracting...

When the couple in our very real world sleeps,
We see them hold each other tight,
Knowing that their children,
Might have Black futures.
I'm still contracting...

And so when a brother and the sister,
Meet in an embrace,
Let us see their Black Love be their unspoken bond,
As siblings we all know.
I'm still contracting...

In this world,
Our world,
There is a love
Which has no bounds...

What if I start expanding?

BLACK NOVA *breaks into song. It is a song of protest. A cacophony of the noise of protest. Of gunshots. Snatches of speeches. Protest songs. Children crying. 'I can't breathe' chants over and over. The office banter. The minstrel song. The stomping of feet. The cry for help, the endless chatter, the National Anthem, the endless clapping.*

6. Out

ROO *and* ORION *stand next to each other, dancing.*

ROO. Sunshine.
  Rays.
  Open sky-blues.
  Endless hope.

  As ROO *slowly moves away from* ORION, LOIS *enters.*

  My skin warmed.
  Heart.
  Bursting.
  The songs from the trees.
  The sweetness of these things…

ORION. You can kind of hear it.
  In between the warbling.
  And the faux-American twang
  Underneath the even faker sense of rhythm /

  Roo!
  Where the fuck are you?
  I don't need this.

ROO. A halo.
  A glow.
  And for sure the heavens are saying hello.
  Maybe it's paradise.

All yellow.
All green.
Everything soft… like
Soft butterfly's wing.
I think that's what it's like…

And I'm looking up at the trees.
And they're glowing.
Like proper glowing.
The greens have turned to gold.
The branches to liquid stalks,
Holding petals of sunshine…

Beat.

ORION *tries to push past a crowd and* LOIS.

LOIS. You alright?
    You lost your mates?
    Or you trying to lose them…

    Laughs –

    Cos same!

ORION. Sorry!
    Alright…
    It's just my sister…
    And I've got to find her.
    She's done a bit too much you know…
    And today is…

LOIS. I'll help you.
    Two is better than one and all that.
    Tell me about her.
    What does she look like?
    What's she wearing?
    What's your name?

ROO. Happy birthday!
    To you…
    You think we would forget?

Never forget.
Never letting you go…

Beat.

But I can't move.
I mean I really can't…
And I think I can hear someone calling me…

ORION. Orion.
Like the constellations…
Don't ask.
And yeah…
Yeah yeah…
Look for a Black woman whose pupils are bigger than the sun…

LOIS. Bigger than the sun?
Yeah I guessed…
Black woman…
Cos you are…
I'll go this way.
And I hope…
Let's meet back here in five…

Can I…?
Give me you number!

ROO. Yeah I'm moving…
That's my feet walking.
And it feels less like…
You know…
Like I'm in a hole…
Digging…

ORION. Green eyes… I think…
Hair… soft…
Teeth… or lips… both.
Nothing special…
Just another face innit…
Just another woman…

LOIS. Man, man, man!
   I was so not cool.
   But man!
   He's fine…
   Like fine fine fine!
   So I'm going, going, gone /

ROO. I've got to get up.
   Got to make my legs work.
   Fuck why do I always have to go too far…
   Orion is going to be pissed.
   But they said it wasn't that strong.
   And I've done more before so…

ORION. Roo!

LOIS. Orion…

ORION. Roo!
   What the fuck?
   I've been looking for you…
   What are you doing?
   Where have you been?
   Aurora Hammond!

LOIS. Hey!
   You found her…
   And I found you /

ROO. Who the fuck is she?
   Orion!
   Is she with you?

LOIS. I'm Lois /

ROO. Like Superman's girlfriend?

ORION. Roo! Damn / (*Nervous laugh.*)

ROO. Am I seeing this for true?
   Or am I still hallucinating?

ORION. No you're tripping.

   They all look at each other and start laughing –

ROO. I was lost in the woods over there.
    Don't know how I got there.
    One minute I was by your side,
    The next I was talking to a fly...
    I mean you should have seen his eyes.
    And he was talking to me...

ORION. Like wow!

    ORION *laughs* –

LOIS. Leave her.
    She's getting in touch with nature.
    Her wild self!

ROO. I can't remember...
    Like it was deep though.
    Like he wanted me to know something really important.

    Like there was something I should know.
    And I kept asking...
    But then I kept forgetting the answer...
    And it was so deep...
    And I was really feeling it...

ORION. What you were feeling was the magic /

ROO. Yes!

ORION. Mushrooms Roo.
    That's what.
    Magic mushrooms!

LOIS. What you don't believe in magic?
    In the endless possibilities of our universe?
    Or the unknown, the unseen /

ROO. Yeah that /

LOIS. And the power of nature to talk to us?
    You don't believe in magic?

ORION. Erm...

LOIS. Cos I believe in magic.

ROO. Yeah!!

LOIS. I believe in the magic of every day.

ROO. It's all around us...

LOIS. In oh so many ways...

ROO. In oh so many ways...

ORION. What the fuck?

ROO. I feel...

> ROO *unstable on her feet – seems to have dozed off –*
> ORION *holds her up –*

ORION. I've got to get her home.
Nice to meet you...

ROO. Maybe a tequila shot will help?

- **We Black-on-Black Love, we skin to skin, we touch heaven and climb back to earth.**

- **Black Love is an ancient dance.**

- **I think Black Love is self-love, undeniably unconditional love. It's something I'm looking forward to experiencing.**

- **When I think of Black Love, I think of peace and safety. I also thing of overcoming obstacles and being a shining role model of what love can be.**

7. Home

ROO *is sat throwing a ball back and forth between her hands.*

ORION *enters. Walks silently over to the other side of the table. Sits. Staring into space.*

Long beat.

Ball keeps being tossed. Back and forth.

ROO. Well?

Beat.

I haven't got all day you know. Don't ask me to wait at home
for some news and then you go all silent…

ORION. Is it?

ROO. Yes.
Seriously /

ORION. I do have some news actually.

ROO. Spill then.

ORION. We got any whiskey?

ROO. What?

Where are we getting whiskey from on our budget?
The day we just casually have whiskey is the day we win the
Lottery. I've got weed though!

ORION. Seen!

ROO. And I'm still here waiting…

ORION. You know that lot /

ROO. Who?

ORION. I got a callback!
This time with real people.
In a real room.
I think they were keen you know /

ROO. Wait what?
Is this what you had me running home for? /

ORION. But I fucked it.

ROO. How? Again…

ROO *kisses her teeth* –

ORION. Rude!

ROO. Or what do you want me to say?
You either want to do this acting thing or not.

I've seen this too many times. You get bare excited about
some audition, spend a load of money on haircuts and new
T-shirts that show your personality, and then you bottle it and
end up getting turned down and cussing everyone in the
industry for about two weeks /

ORION. Don't hold back yeah /

ROO. I just don't get it.

Do something else. There's so many other things you could
be doing that would really bring you some sense of
satisfaction you know. This acting thing clearly isn't it.
That's all I'm saying /

ORION. I fucked it because I think I was asking too many
questions. Like I basically said to them that I am not about
that life of playing a fucking White woman's puppet or
whatever fucking fantasy the writer has decided she wants to
share /

ROO. Wait… you told them that?

Beat.

I'm proud of you Orion.
Is that actually my bruv though!
We have to stand up to this shit now.
Nuff a nuff!

Moves to hug ORION *tight* –

Sorry I was… you know…

ORION. Anyway he liked my passion /

ROO. Really?

ORION. Anyway they want me to… you know… I think…

ROO *reaches into a drawer and pulls out a single party
popper. Walks to stand in front of* ORION. *Pulls it. Pop!* –

ROO. We have to celebrate!
You cussed them out and that needs celebrating!
Where should we go? /

ORION. I'm going out!

ROO. Still…

ORION. I'm going out.

ROO. Right…

Beat.

ORION. It's a work thing. I said I'd pop in.

ROO. I've come to those things with you plenty.

ORION. I need to change Roo.

Beat.

Roo?

Beat.

ROO. What?

Beat.

What do you want from me?
A whole song?

ORION. You sounded so like Mum then…

ROO. Remember the way she used to cuss Dad out if he played
a trick on her.
Oh my days remember when he put that big plastic snake
just under one of the cushions. And she freaked out and
screamed like she'd seen a ghost /

ORION. 'Let me tell you something right here and now you
think what you doing is a joke. Yeah. You think you're
funny. A real joker yeah. The joke is on you because your
ankles ashy like used coal so you go laugh at someone else.
And get out of my house. Go eat someone else food tonight.'

ROO. And then he would turn on the charm –

ORION. 'The way your lips curl up like that when you talk
Cyn. It like God painted them lips himself.'

ROO. And her screw-face like –

'Well I pity you because this is the last time you gon ever have anything to do with these lips unless I'm telling this whole street what a good-for-nothing' /

ORION. And then he would walk over to the record player like this innit –

ORION *skanks across the room miming the action of someone placing a needle on a record –*

ROO. Something real smooth yeah like Gregory Abbott…

ORION. Dancing –

And then he would do that dance towards her /

ROO. And you could see her just… just… and… and she would just…

They are both dancing separately –

ORION. Then we would have to leave the room cos…

ROO. Proper shameful behaviour you know!

They both giggle – the giggle falls to silence – the silence falls to sadness – the sadness falls heavy –

ORION *moves towards* ROO –

ROO. I'm just…
I know you'll get to do whatever it is you want to do one day Or.
It's just got to be on our terms.
For us.
About *us*.
Not some fuckeries they've created that we have to fit into.

I'm proud of you for today you know…

ORION. I've got to do whatever it takes Roo.
And things like this come with it…

So you'll make me a toasted cheese thingy.
Let's use that machine more than once a year.

ORION *exits – but can still be heard – a different rythmn –*

Song: 'Constellations'

ROO.
Aurora and Orion
Constellations in time
More than blood
More than just fam

ORION. Sister, sister, sister!

ROO.
Don't know this life without you
Don't know this world without us

ROO *is still dancing to the beat of their song –*
She moves to a drawer – gets a box out –
ROO *sits at a table – starts to roll a joint –*

8.

BLACK NOVA *enters.*

BLACK NOVA.
This is the best thing.
The bit between the other things.
The moment when this time is beyond now time.
The bit that feels almost…

The word won't come…

This is the good bit.
Where we lift off the ground,
Like a single leaf,
The wind promising an adventure,
A different view.

So we let it take us.
And it doesn't disappoint.

Your own person.
High on your...

The word won't come...

And this is beyond them.
Beyond their grip.
Beyond their questions.
This bit is...
Happy and weightless.

And this is the best thing,
This good bit,
This spot-beyond-them thrill,

It feels like...
I'm just wanting to say it...

The word won't come...

It feels like...

And the thing is...
It never lasts long enough.
Because there is no...

The word won't come...

Is the word even real?

It's not there in the chase.
In the chase all you're doing is running.
Away from their hold.
Away from those questions.

There is no...

The word won't come...

It is real isn't it?

Freedom.

BLACK NOVA *quivers* –

That's what this thing is...
Like a language all of its own.

You've got to taste it under your tongue to find it.
Push down your hand down into your belly for the shape
of it.
Tear apart your heart to reach it…

FREEDOM!!!!

BLACK NOVA *runs in endless circles with the joy of it.*

BLACK NOVA *song breaks into the space. It is a song of
protest. A cacophony of the noise of protest. Of gunshots.
Snatches of speeches. Protest songs. Children crying. 'I can't
breathe' chants over and over. The office banter. The minstrel
song. The stomping of feet. The cry for help, the endless
chatter, the National Anthem, the endless clapping.*

PART TWO

1. Restaurant

A table with candles and wine.

ORION *and* LOIS *sit on either side of it. They stare in each other's eyes.*

Song: 'Speechless'

ORION.
Looking over at you…

LOIS.
Something's taken over me…

ORION.
I just can't find the words…

LOIS.
Don't know where to begin

ORION.
And it seems no matter what I do…

LOIS.
All the words I had have gone

CHORUS.
You've left me speechless
Speechless
Tongue-tied
Tongue-tied
Completely
Undone inside
Undone inside
I don't know

LOIS.
I…

ORION.
What to say…

                        Don't…

Where to go…

                        Know…

What to do…

                        Why…

Only you make me…

                        I'm…

Speechless…

                        Speechless
                        So where do we go from
                        here?

You've got me on lockdown
And I don't want to be free…

                        I won't ever be the same…

Addicted to your vibe

                        My body wants nobody else

And I'm so glad that you're here

CHORUS.
You've left me speechless
Speechless
Tongue-tied
Tongue-tied
Completely
Undone inside
Undone inside
I don't know

                        LOIS.
                          I…

ORION.
What to say…

Don't…

Where to go…

Know…

What to do…

Why…

Only you make me…

I'm…

Speechless…

Speechless
I just want hold you tight

And you look so good tonight…

Cos you shine so bright and
right…

So let me take you home…

Love you through the
night…

Lady I'm yours…

A dream I dare to dream…

A feeling I never had

CHORUS.
You've left me speechless
Speechless
Tongue-tied
Tongue-tied
Completely
Undone inside
Undone inside
I don't know

LOIS.
I…

ORION.
What to say…

Don't…

Where to go…

Know…

What to do…

Why…

Only you make me…

I'm…

Speechless…

Speechless
So where do we go from
here?

We could go to mine…

You sure…

Nothing I want more

I'm intoxicated just by…

Feel unsteady and I'm not sick
Come on let's do this…

Come on let's do this…

The words I long to hear

hear

2. Home

ORION *and* LOIS.

ORION. So I'm not pretending,
    That I'm not feeling good.
    Spending a night together…
    It's more than out of this world /

LOIS. More and more and more I say,
    This can't be true
    I've found that perfect fit
    For all I've got to give.
    And now I'm here,
    Looking at everything I wanted /

ORION. And standing here next to you
    Makes me sure of what I need
    And it's been worth the waiting and waiting
    The endless hoping /

LOIS. And I just want to remember these sweet sweet kisses.
    The way you held my hand.
    Things we said tonight…
    Never want to forget.
    Can't we just go back to that dance?

ORION. And I can't pretend,
    That I'm not feeling good.
    This night spent together…
    Feels more than one thing.

    ROO *enters*.

ROO. Orion!

ORION. Roo?

ROO. I brought you flowers.

    ROO *holds out a bunch of very sad-looking hand-dragged flowers –*

    For you!

ORION. Can we have one Friday night when you're not coming in like this?

You look like shit.
Where have you been?
Looks like you've been rolling in shit.

ROO. Things got raucous pon the dance floor if you know what I mean...

Pleasure activism is real!

ORION. What?

ROO. The necessity to love beyond our means. To. Take. The. Most. Pleasure. From. Justice and Liberation. To move beyond the confines of struggle. To find another language. To make it not just about the work of it, but to make it about the joy of it. The love of it. The feel-yourself-in-your-body of it. The actual touch-up-yourself of it. The pussyhole enjoyment of it. And get wasted on it. Revel in the community of it. Laugh in the face of it. Find the beauty of it. Let the sucking of a mango be a part of it. Let them see the juice of it run down your chin as you laugh at it. Let it be known that you're tasting the sweetness of it. To realise that there are no parts of us that naturally align with the struggle and the pain of it, and that the pain of it is part of the trick of it and the trick of it is part of death of us /

A noise from somewhere unseen.

What was that? /

ORION. I can't keep telling you to get it together like this. We're grown now.

Get it together!

ROO. That was something /

ORION. Something outside probably.
I'm going back to bed.

No tunes!

ROO. I miss Mum.

Beat.

ORION. I'll take you out for breakfast tomorrow.
To that café in the park.
I know you and Mum used to go there sometimes.

ROO. You're like literally the best brother.

ORION. I know.

Go to bed Roo.

ORION *exits, turning off the lights again –*

ROO *tries to undress. Tripping over her jeans. She gives up.
She collapses in a heap on the floor –*

ROO. And I know you're here with me Mum.
Somewhere.
Teddy Pendergrass running through your lips.
Somehow.
And I can see you and him.
Late-night dancing.
Thinking we're asleep.
Me watching though.
Through the slats of the banisters.
Watching.
Late-night cuffing.
And you're close.
Are you going to proper haunt me /

LOIS *enters.*
ROO *welps in shock –*

LOIS. Hi!

ROO. Who da…? /

LOIS. Sorry…

ROO. You're from that festival…

LOIS. Yeah I helped your brother find you.

I'm glad you remember me…

ROO. And you're here because…

LOIS. I got thirsty.

Long beat.

The two women's eyes fixed on each other –

I'm just getting some water…

LOIS *exits for a beat –*
The sound of a tap running –
LOIS *re-enters –*

Beat.

See you in the morning!

LOIS *exits.*

ROO. Becky with the bland hair?
In my actual abode?
Wearing Mum's…
What kind of fuckeries is happening here?
And how has this caucasity occurred?

ROO *lies down –*
Beat.

How am I meant to sleep now?
Knowing she is in there doing what exactly…
How?
I'm pissed and vex.
Sleep averse.
Can't rest.
Can't…

- **It comes with so much beauty but also the struggle of facing a world that doesn't want it to exist.**

- **As soon as I read the words 'Black Love' I thought of 'Turn Your Lights Down Low' and the lyrics of that song came in my head: 'Turn your lights down low, wo-oh, / Never never try to resist, oh no! / Ooh, let my love ooh, let my love come** tumbling in, / Into our life again, / Oh, I want to give you some good, good lovin' (good, good lovin').'

- **Black Love is our understanding of we in the form of unsaid words, those that need no explanation. It's a freedom to love freely.**

- **Black Love is love. It is a rhythm developed in trust that follows a beat that finds its timing even when one player falls out of sync with the other sometimes.**

3. Out

LOIS *sat at a table*.

ORION *enters*.

LOIS. Excuse waiter!

ORION. Hello madam.

LOIS. I think I would like a coffee, followed by piece of cake. Something sweet…
Like extremely fine piece of beautiful Black man, with a side of extremely impressive back and crack /

ORION. Yo! You can't say that here!

Don't get me wrong it's nice to see you and…

LOIS. Just came to see where my man was working.

ORION. Cool. Cool.
I can't talk for too long…
Actually we're about to open.

LOIS. Yes well you won't have to do this for long.
That new acting thing you're waiting on… I got a good feeling about it!
Like I've seen shit in theatre that's been well crap…
Watching that short film you showed me…
You're fiyah… they'll see!

ORION. Yeah not sure about it still…
     This actually pays the rent… and like we're lucky Dad sorted
     us with the flat but you know money worries isn't worth it /

LOIS. You're actually tripping!
     You're so good. You have to do it.
     Like that's your dream right? /

ORION. You can't say I'm good, you haven't even seen me /

LOIS. You showed me that recording of your college play. You
     were basically on another level from everyone else /

ORION. Was /

LOIS. No no. Not into that energy /

ORION. What? I'm just saying /

LOIS. I can help you with your profile thing… what's it called?

ORION. Spotlight.

LOIS. Yeah and we'll go see stuff and like let's make this
     happen. I'm on your side with this. You're good Or /

ORION. Don't let Roo hear you call me that /

LOIS. A friend of mine's a photographer he can do new photos
     for you.
     Trust me on this.
     You cannot waste this talent /

ORION. You think?

LOIS. Listen I'm going to call my mate now about the photos.
     This isn't for you /

ORION. Maybe…

LOIS. Don't be one of those Black men that's always down on
     themselves and shit and playing the race card. Making
     excuses about why they're not making shit happen. That's
     just not attractive.
     Get yours!

     LOIS *starts doing a dance as though dashing money –*

ORION. Get mines!

LOIS. So waiter… let me tell you about the boyfriend.
He's a very… exceptionally talented Black actor and he is doing *thangs*.

ORION. Is it?

Beat.

Oh shit. I got to get on.

ORION *moves to exit* –

LOIS. See you at yours yeah?

4. Home

ORION *is sat alone*.

ROO *enters*.

ORION. There's fresh coffee.

ROO. I don't want coffee.

ORION. I can make you tea then.

Beat.

You okay?
Did you go out *again* last night?

ROO. Yeah I am feeling sick right about now.
Qwhite sick.

Beat.

ORION. I've got a call from that company. They've booked me.
I've got to get these lines down…

Beat.

Roo…

ROO *moves to walk past* ORION –
ORION *grabs her by the arm* –

So what you're still not talking to me?
It's been days of the silent treatment and I'm done with it
you know /

ROO. Oh now you want my opinion?

ORION. We usually just talk.
Always.
That's how it is /

ROO. Let me be bruv!
You do you.
And *her.*
And I'll do whatever.

ORION. What's this about?
I've found someone I like...
And if it was you...
I'd be happy for you /

ROO. You can't see it?
If this was 'how it should be'.
What you should do...
I'd be happy for you too /

ORION. Then be that!
See it for what it is,
Don't take what's sweet and make it taste bitter.
If this was you /

ROO. This could never be me.
I could never do this...
Take liberties with our history.
You see that don't you?

ORION. See what?
It feels good to be with someone I get on with.
What's the problem you're seeing?

ROO. What's happened to you?
That *woman* is not who...

What…
That's not what we are!

ORION. Are you serious right now?
Is this for real?
Or are you just playing with me?
Love is love /

ROO. Love?
Since when?
After how long?
It must be good…
Like she must know some *tricks*!

ORION. Fuck you!
It's deeper than that.
We have a connection /

ROO. You've been meeting her in secret.
Taking her places where you can't be seen…
Yes I see the connection…
And leaving me in the dark…

ORION. For fuck's sake!

You're a child you know that!

ROO. And you've been pussy-blinded.

Beat.

ORION *pulls his phone out of his pocket –*

Song: 'Deleting My Sadness'

ORION.
You see this?
This is me deleting my sadness
No more swiping right or left
Saying 'Hey' to strange faces
Blind dates made in hell
Clean shirt won't dispel
Hair not quite right
And no time to shave

You see that?
That is desperation avoided
Over-sweating
Ashy hands
Check breath
Smile loaded
A meal set for two…
Or what are you?
A wasteman with no clue or class!

Those days are gone
I have moved on
Here's me deleting my sadness
My sadness

A lonely walk
After no-tongues-please kiss
A gaping hole in that clean shirt
Where loneliness exists
Endless nights awake
Waiting you know
Waiting to know…
If you might be good enough
If she thinks you got the right stuff

Those days are gone
I have moved on
Here's me deleting my sadness
My sadness
I'm getting clear of the madness
It's madness
I want to stay in my gladness
My gladness
Here's me deleting my sadness

Beat.

ORION *kisses his teeth –*

I'm going out.

ROO. Well I'm staying in!

Orion!

And by the way you're a prick!

Don't ever let her wear *anything* of Mum's again!

5. Out – audition

ORION *stands*.

ORION. It's not that you can't love me.
It's that you won't love me.
It's that you're not even trying to love me.
Don't listen to what they have to say.
What do they know?
They are not us.
They do not feel the love that we feel.
Say something goddamn it!
Can't you see you're driving me crazy?

Did you like the peonies?

What?

Flowers.
Can't you see how much I want you?
I'm here spilling my guts out to you.
I'm human too.
I am flesh and blood.
Can't you see that?
I'm just a man with a great big heart…
And all I want is you.
Say you want me too?

Again?
Definitely…

More threatening?
Is he actually angry with her though?

Do what you have to do to get where you want to get…

Did you like the peonies?

Peonies? Why?

Nothing. Sorry.

Beat.

I thought you wanted us to be together.

I can do more…
So much more if you want.
I just don't want to be a slave…

I wonder if they've noticed too?

My love?
Yes it is…
Complicated…

Right…

Violent…

Don't remember reading that in the casting brief!
I've got to hold it down…
Think about it…
Check yourself Orion…

I'm more of a lover than a fighter…

Beat.

Yes yes of course!

Okay.

Beat.

6. Home

ROO *is sat on the ground by candlelight. She has a kind of shrine of objects and crystals in a circle in front of her. An incense stick burns.*

- **Black Love is the deep comfort of being with someone who understands your experience without needing everything explained and decoded.**

Song: 'Incense Check'

ROO.
Incense check
Crystals check
Spirits come through
When things go crazy like properly crazy
And I don't know what to do
I open up to you
Goddess
Black and Brown
Ancient wise women and ancestors alike
I call you to bring me wisdom and joy
Bring me hope and light
In this darkness
Darkness

Yemoja, beautiful, mother to all
Bring me a softer heart
Let me feel your touch touch

What am I supposed to do Yemoja?
Help me to find my way through

Incense check
Crystals check
Spirits come through
When things go crazy like properly crazy
And I don't know what to do
I open up to you

Hoping to
Find the truth /

ORION *and* LOIS *enter – turning the lights on.*
ROO, *shocked, jumps to her feet –*

ROO. What the fuck Orion?
Why are you back so early? /

ORION. I live here.

ROO. Yes I know but…

ROO *gestures at* LOIS –

ORION. Didn't think you'd be in. Friday nights are usually your crazy time /

ROO. Well we're all trying different things these days /

LOIS. Didn't realise you were spiritual.

ROO. –

LOIS. I don't know you know.
It's sort of…
Don't you think all that hippy 'goddesses and crystals' shit is a bit…
It's a bit off /

ROO. Off?

Okay…

LOIS. What are you reaching for?

ROO. I'm reaching?
Guess you're knowing things that I don't know /

ORION. It was a small comment Roo.

LOIS. Look I think all this new spirituality and tarots and candles and everything…
It's all the same mumbo-jumbo as that lot on Glastonbury.
They want people to buy into all these candles with Egyptian symbols and African *queens* on and jewellery to make money…

And that's fucked up you know…
And as Black women we have to watch for all that
capitalism dressed up…

ROO. What did you just say?
AS BLACK WOMEN!

ORION. Roo stop!

LOIS. I didn't mean /

ROO. Oh I get it now.

You have Rachel Dolezal-itis!

ORION. Seriously?

ROO. Well if the shoe fits…

LOIS. It was a slip of the tongue /

ROO. You didn't slip on nothing but your own truth.
Or maybe they're just lies you have to tell yourself every
day?

LOIS. I was talking about all women and the last time I checked
I was a woman!
And I'm not the one sat in the dark telling myself lies /

ORION. Listen yeah this is all a bit…
Why don't we just all chill because we have to get on now
you know /

ROO. Do we?

LOIS. It's all good.
I get why you don't like me.
But it's not like that! I've gone out with Asian men, White
men and my first boyfriend was Chinese you know.
But yeah I like the Brown-skin swagger but…

ROO. Listen to the way you're talking Lois.
Did you parents in Cambridge*shire* teach you to talk like that?
No.
Did your older cousin talk like that?
No.

I don't give a shit what kind of Benetton relationship history
you've had.
Or how far you scrape your hair back.

And were you talking about how women are being exploited
when it's your lot on some hill in Glastonbury Pagan-
dancing for Summer Solstice?

I DON'T CARE WHAT YOUR WHITE FEMINISM HAS
TO TELL ME!
It's said enough already.
Too much.
Too little.
Always on us.
Never too near though.
Cos yours is a bigger fight.
Right?
No.

I just don't see you respecting what's not yours!
Some things are sacred.
Should be kept out of *your* mouth.
This is my culture not yours /

LOIS. Yours? /

ROO. Don't fucking interrupt!
    Listen…
    Someone needs to slap some sense /

ORION. No!
    Enough.
    This is out of order Roo.
    Why do you think I'm with her?
    She's not some English-rose wannabe.
    She knows things /

ROO. What?
    What does she know Or?
    And you…
    You can't see how you are disrespecting what our own mum
    and dad taught us?
    This skin /

LOIS. I should go…

ORION. No.
　Stay.

　That was *them*.
　Then.
　This is us…

ROO. And who made us?

　That Black man.
　That Black woman.
　You are a Black man too.
　And I am a Black woman /

LOIS. Yes you said!

　ROO *moves quickly towards* LOIS –
　ORION *holds her back just in time* –

ORION. Please.

　No!

ROO. You think you know what there is to know about us.
　Say those words through gritted teeth…
　Cos you can't be what we are.
　Cos you don't see what we carry…

　It's not about your sense of dress or the way you shade your
　face.
　This is a history that you wish you could bear /

ORION. Chill Roo.

LOIS. I said something and I thought you would take it lightly /

ROO. On my mother's grave /

ORION. What you doing?

　Roo Mum wouldn't want to see us like this.

ROO. Are you sure?

　Beat.

ORION. And why can't I choose who I get to be with?

Black women are hard work /

ROO. That's what you're actually saying /

ORION. Wait I'm not the only one who thinks it.
They want too much.
And you're never good enough.
They want a man to provide but not to speak up too much.
Taking the piss with all these demands.
Ball-grinding.
Head-twisting.
Face-screwing.
Too much of a headache.
Not enough to enjoy.
Always comparing us to a metric that isn't even real.
Wanting a man street like Kano,
But with the Ps like Raheem Sterling.
No.
We can't be all of that.
And then more.
I'm looking for an easy life and nothing else.
That's what we're all realising.
Being with a Black woman is like…
All the games without the fun.
All the chase without the win.

ROO. You actually said those things out loud?

ORION. There are things you don't know /

ROO. Every day watching their Black Love grow…

ORION. –

ROO. I think you should go.

Beat.

(*Shouting.*) I need you to go away from me!

ORION *and* LOIS *reluctantly exit.*

- **Black Love is that... deep belly laugh, deep healing, deep strokes, deep red, smoky jollof rice, deep healing, deep-sea diving, deep roots in deep soil, deep activism, deep restoration. Deep.**

- **It's not just being with another Black person, it's a shared love of your Blackness.**

7.

BLACK NOVA *enters.*

    Song: 'Bones Broken'

BLACK NOVA.
That sound...

Listen...

That's the sound of my bones breaking
Took two of them to hold me down and another to shout in my ear –

IT'S ALWAYS THE WRONG WORDS!
WHY ARE YOU HERE?

Where are you really from?

And the blood drains from my heart...
Usually it would take a tiny explosion of miracles for that to happen
Usually...
They would ask me those questions...
I would run...
They would chase...
Usually...
The game is enough
But now it seems it is not
Let's change the rules...

They want to catch me in nets sewn with wire –
With hands dripping with trinkets dug out of the earth –
Damn fine earth with imperial names
But they're no longer interested in my answers to their
questions
They've asked enough times and not heard what they wanted
Now their happiness comes from gazing at me

So they catch me
And my bones are broken
Scrape my tongue of any words they don't understand and
they just want to gaze
Say pretty things…
Such pretty things…
Such broken wings…

I have already started to expand and that's the problem. And
I don't know how to stop now…
What I would give for contraction…

And when they can't find what more they can take they let me
go
So here I am…

Expanding…
Trying my hand at freedom
Bones broken

But where did this all start?

BLACK NOVA *lays down –*

8.

ROO *and* ORION *stand apart – somehow in the same space –*
somehow separate.

ROO. I was five. I think. The memory has me smaller than the
average car…

ORION. It was in a park.
That time during winter's grip when the cold is not eager to leave but the sun is definitely showing its face…

ROO. I was on my bike for only the third time ever. Magical and powerful.

BLACK NOVA *enters*.

BLACK NOVA. Those wheels were turning…

ORION. Somehow I had got in with the cool kids. I was cool.
And there's a girl, and I was smoking.
And shitting it!
If my mum…

ROO. I look back and up and I can see Dad's face so handsome.
His hands are reaching out to me… like if he needed to, he could just pull me back with some invisible rope…

BLACK NOVA. But that invisible rope isn't real…

ORION. And home is far away in my mind…
Here and now is everything. This girl is everything.

ROO. And the wheels are turning fast…
And I'm heading for the road…

ORION. That day without warning, some time between drag of smoke and ash,
This girl is holding my hand…

ROO. I can't stop and my feet aren't even on the pedals any more.
If I am screaming, you can hardly hear it from the noise the wheels are making…

ORION. And as the sun is fighting its own battle of the day,
I am looking at her pale white skin, holding on to my hand so tight.

ROO. There's nothing that we can do now cos the motion is on, on and on…
I hit a parked car like a bag of bones.

ORION. I'm going out with a White girl you know. And people
know.

And people stare but *I'm* feeling kind of…

ROO. But the pain is coming slow, and my father is coming
fast.

But before he gets there a White woman passing by…
She stops and looks down on me…

ORION. I feel… to say things that I feel to her…
I say things that I want for the first time that I'm thinking
them…

ROO. You can't be running wild like that in this country.
You need a leash child. A short leash.

BLACK NOVA. And I'm on a short fuse!

ORION. The first time I say I love you is to this White girl. And
I kiss her white hands…

I look at her and I am thinking I can find love for myself
here.

ROO. And everything in me is hurting.
Five years old you know, and I already know that *that*
woman is looking at me *different*…

ORION. And I see a way that I can be less different.
She is maybe my ticket to some other thing…

ROO. And I'm looking at her Whiteness and… all she can see
is my Blackness… and…

BLACK NOVA *exits*.

ORION *exits*.

ROO *sits alone* –

Song: 'Mama Tell Me'

ROO.
Mama tell me like only you know how
Yes I'm listening
Properly listening

Whose image am I made in
God knows what I mean
Which hands will I grow into

I'm done fighting what will never be
Done caressing the wounded parts of me
When do I get to live my life
Wholly live my dreams

Mama tell me like only you know how
Yes I'm listening
Properly listening

They say it takes time to find your place
Your step, this flow, that beat
For some it takes much more

An eternity of waiting, inhaling
Never blowing it out
Falling
Fading

When do I get to live my life
Wholly live my dreams

Mama tell me like only you know how

CHORUS.
Done fighting what can't be…

ROO.
Yes I'm listening
Properly listening

CHORUS.
Done caressing the wounded parts of me…

ROO.
I'm done with expecting
Expecting things to change

CHORUS.
Done fighting who I am…

ROO.
I'm done with accepting these silly games

CHORUS.
And all I can be…

ROO.
Mama done told me just like she does
Yes I've been listening
Listened too long

I'm moving on up
Taking space for me
Black Love surrounds me
So I'm creating my own destiny
My own destiny
My own destiny
My own destiny

9.

ORION *stands alone.*

ORION. What is it you want from me?

Am I not allowed to have dreams, hopes, ambitions too?
You want me to be endlessly quarrelling with myself about
what you might be saying… doing… and what?
I'm meant to keep looking over my shoulder. Waiting for the
bullet real or imagined to come my way.

I want this thing…

I have someone who believes I can do it. Do you know what
it means to hear that? To believe…

And who gets to say what I can be or not be?
Who cares if the words don't resonate?
Is this not the point?
Escape from this me and be someone else…

I've got this you know. I can do this and she…

She's not lying…

These dreams man… they're making me mad keeping them inside. It's making me lose my grip on what is, and trying to pretend my dreams aren't speaking to me every day. So yeah I'm going to pretend…

Switch it up!

Play it like it should be…

And at the end of the day, does it matter what you want from me? If I'm giving the people what they want… does any of it really matter?

I matter… and she…

Doesn't that even matter?

Fuck it.

I'm going around in these circles for what?

When do I get to choose?

- **It's true that love is blind, but building a solid relationship takes more than love alone. Love is subjective, an interpretation of emotions, and for me Black Love is the meaning of relationship that makes most sense.**

- **When people talk about Black Love, to me I think of my Grandmum (actually my great-grandmother but everyone just called her Grandmum)… If I could distill it into a word it would be 'Grandmum'. In a sentence or two, I would say… Every single man in my family has run away from a troubled home and to find solace, plantain and a clip round the ear from Grandmum because she was, is and always will be the Bernards.**

PART THREE

1. Out-out

A party is happening.
ORION *and* LOIS *standing, both dressed in seventies fancy dress.*
They look around them.

Long beat.

ORION. Sorry.

LOIS. I get it.
Really I do Or.
You can talk to me you know.

ORION. Why don't you go in?
It's way more fun in there.

Anyways my cousins love telling people embarrassing
stories about me /

LOIS. I'll stay out here with you.

Your Uncle Derek is very touchy-feely.

ORION. Did he tell you he had to be really close because of his
eyesight?

LOIS. Yeah.

ORION. Man can see everything clearly.

LOIS. Ugh no way!

They both start to laugh –

ROO *– also dressed in seventies fancy dress – enters.*

A popular song from the 1970s seeps into the space –

ORION. Roo…

I didn't think you were…

I mean Auntie Chrissy would have killed you if you didn't come to her 'Fab Fifty' seventies party.

Beat.

LOIS. Want a drink Or?
 Roo?

ORION. –

LOIS. Okay.
 I'll go in.

 Nice to see you Roo /

ROO. My name is Aurora!

 LOIS *exits.*

ORION. For fuck's sake where are you staying?
 How can I not know where you are?
 You're not answering my calls /

ROO. I don't get to tell you what to do with your life so you don't get to tell me what to do with mine.

 Beat.

 I'm fine…

ORION. Mum always warned me about when a woman says 'I'm fine.'

 Laughs awkwardly –

 Beat.

 How's things?

ROO. Wearing these ridiculous clothes.

ORION. You look like…
 I mean it's nice…
 It kind of reminds me of /

ROO. Donna Summer on a bad day.

 Beat.

Listen…
I don't want to chat to you and your girlfriend.
I can't do any of this any more /

ORION. And you have to move back.
That was the deal with the flat.
Dad bought it for the both of us…

ROO. I won't tell him if you don't.

ROO moves to leave –

ORION. The rehearsals are going really well.

ROO. Right.

ORION. They're saying it might transfer to America or
something.
I could be in actual New York!

ROO. Seen.

ORION. I am fucking hungry to do something different.

Roo…

LOIS enters.

LOIS. Your aunt is cutting the cake and she wants everyone
inside!

Beat.

LOIS exits.

ORION. Come home.

ROO. Go eat your cake!

Beat.

ORION. You took all of Mum's things.

ROO. No. You did!

ORION. What?

ROO. When I saw her wearing that…

It's not just things Orion. It's *her* things. It's things that have the smell of her history. Her body. Her softness and you don't feel a way about giving that away?

Beat.

ORION. What do I have to do?

ROO. Nothing. Do nothing.

ORION. It's not all on me to fix this…

ROO. No. It's always on us.
We have to heal things. Make things right again. Say the right things. Make everyone feel better.
Who is protecting us? Saying the right things so the shit doesn't cut as deep. Who's making this…
This fucking everyday pain go away?
Not trying on for size but actually respecting it.
Instead of expecting people to be constantly shifting in the reality of their existence just to you know *live*!

ORION. What you think I don't know about that any more?
I'm not pretending to be Black.
Nothing has changed about me Roo.
Nothing is different /

ROO. You're on some very different shit.
How am I meant to not hear what I hear?
Have Black women in my flat celebrating themselves and then walk straight into you and her.
These things don't gel…

ORION. Seriously?
Because of who I'm fucking I don't get it?
If you don't want her there some nights just say /

ROO. It's not about that Orion.
It's about what you're giving her permission to think you know…
How she was talking to me…
How she's still moving mad…
She wants all the 'vibe' without the hard work of just holding your head. Lifting your head up.

Things have changed for us /

ORION. Us?
Even you saying those words feels...

ROO. The truth is hard yeah but I have to protect what's ours.
What's theirs /

ORION. Do you know why Dad left Mum?
It wasn't some shiny perfect Wakanda love.
They had arguments.
And sometimes Mum would blank him for days.
And sometimes he left for days too.
And when we were in the market nuff White women would
say hello to him in a particular way...
It took me years to recognise that look but when I did...
I knew where he spent those nights.
What's in your head isn't real.

ROO. They stood for something.	ORION. And that's just the way it is.
I don't need you to explain that	
They weren't perfect.	
I get that!	*Brother and sister*
	Black Love like no other
	Take what you will but don't
	give me another sister

2. Out

ORION *stands alone – feeling very alone.*

ORION.
We're all getting on so well.
Like a whole little family.

I hate it here.

Week one and two have been amazing really…
Really feels like we're in the right place going into week three…

> *The absolutely longest days of my life.*

Oh right.
Why are you thinking about cutting that?

> *What did I just hear?*

It's my big scene.

Right so she's asked you to look at that?

> *Like what the fuck!*

She doesn't believe her character would ever find someone subservient to her attractive?

> *So all the babies that were born to slave traders aren't real then?*
> *Like all these men didn't beat those women with one hand and stroke their titties with the other?*

Beat.

I would really love us all to have a chat about this. I think it would be good for me to hear what she feels…

> *My girl better start talking cos…*

Afraid? Afraid of what? Me?
Oh right.
Do you think I've done anything to give her the impression she should be afraid of me?

Beat.

> *And you're going to leave me hanging – making out I've imagined it all?*

I know you're not saying that but we've all been having some really great conversation in the room you know…
I mean I kind of get intimate with her…

> *And trust me that shit isn't easy.*
> *It's the snorting...*

And yeah if you feel you want to change things I guess it's up to the writer...

Wait.
What?
Is it?
She's her flatmate?

Beat.

No no I know it's not like that...

> *IT IS EXACTLY LIKE THAT!*

> *And now I'm here in this room,*
> *On my own with this...*
> *My throat dry, mouth open wide.*
> *So there's one more tactic to try...*
> *Let the appeasing begin.*

It's still about serving the story right?
I mean it's more believable maybe if she doesn't... you know...
It's the power dynamic right?

Maybe not power...
Some other word...
I mean you know... it's just how these things are seen aren't they...

Beat.

Yes yes I have a girlfriend...

Yeah she's White.

> *Fuck!*

ORION *is raging – he runs around – directionless / confused / searching.*

Stops.

Beat.

ORION *stands looking at his feet*.

Yeah…

I don't really know what else to say…

Yes I get that.
I would feel disappointed too.

> *But you know this stuff is kind of…*
> *It's kind of burning through my soul.*

Like I don't know what to do with it but…
I don't know if kissing another White woman is really saying what you want it to say you know…

I don't know if it's really going to make the world that you want us to believe in.

> *Do you even know the world you're living in?*

Right…

It's not even real…
And what you're selling us…

> *What we're selling day in and day…*
> *It's…fucked…*

Beat.

But I get it…
That's what we're doing here.
Right?

To sell *dreams*.

> *I can't sell your dream…*
> *And I mean I tried to…*
> *For real…*

I did.
Every day…
But I'm not buying what you're selling…

Laughs –

How does that make you feel?
Hearing me say no to your version of me…

No.
No!
Don't turn away.

This is not hate speech.
This is real.
That's what we're doing.
And I don't have to be selling something unhealthy…
Untrue…
To sanitise what?

I don't always have to kiss White women.

Peonies.

I don't always have to kiss White women.

Peonies.

I don't always have to kiss White women.

Peonies.

I don't always have to kiss White women.

Peonies.

Laughs –

ROO *enters.*

ROO. Okay great!

That sound… Listen… That's the sound of my bones breaking.

IT'S ALWAYS THE WRONG WORDS!

ORION. WHY ARE YOU HERE?

ROO. WHERE ARE YOU REALLY FROM?

Song: 'Bones Broken'

And the blood drained from
my heart
Usually it would take small
explosions
Of miracles to make that
happen
Usually they would ask me
those questions
I would run
They would chase
Usually the game is
enough
…Still here
Let's change the rules

They want to catch me and
keep me in a cage
Hands dripping with
trinkets dug out of the
earth
Damn fine earth with
imperial names
Couldn't care about the
answers to their questions
So they catch me and my
bones are broken
Scrape my tongue of any
words they don't know
They just want to gaze
Say pretty things
Such pretty things
Such broken wings
And they want to just gaze
Say pretty things
Such pretty things
Such broken wings

BLACK NOVA. I buried
  myself.
  Deep.
  Deep in some hole in their
  ground.
  In the Blackest of black
  earth.
  Don't ask me how deep
  because I am done with
  Questions.

Ask me where.
Ask me where is so deep
that my eyes can't cry.
Blackity Blackness.
That's where.
I buried myself so deep this
time…

I have to keep my hand on
my heart just to know I'm
not dead…

3. Home

LOIS *sits on the floor – in the semi-darkness of a candlelit room. She has all the paraphernalia of* ROO*'s spiritual practice spread out in front of her. Some weird African music plays in the background.*

ORION *enters.*
He looks around the room.

ORION. Lois!

He turns the music off –

LOIS. I didn't hear you come in /

ORION *watches* LOIS *get up and put a light on –*

ORION. I didn't think that was your thing…

LOIS. Just wanted to you know… there's something calming…

ORION. Right…

LOIS. And I'm not doing it to buy into some nonsense though…

ORION. That's Roo's!
I'm not sure you should be /

LOIS. I won't tell her if you don't.

ORION. Or maybe just not touch her things.

Beat.

LOIS. You've been in rehearsals all this time?

ORION. Decided to walk it back.

LOIS. You look tired.
Let me make you some food.
Bought some plantain and ackee today.

She laughs –

You should have seen the shopkeeper's face.
Looked at me like –

– 'What's a White girl like you buying food like that?'

I looked at her, and picked up a handful of Scotch bonnet.
Didn't say anything obviously.
Just looked at her straight in her face, and kept her guessing.

Beat.

ORION. Did she actually do anything to you?

LOIS. No but I know what she's thinking /

ORION. Do you?
I mean that could be seen as…

LOIS. She was kind of giving me a dirty look.
You know…
How do *you* say it?
Screw-face!

Beat.

ORION. Need to learn some lines.
Got a lot to do…

LOIS. So rehearsal was good?

Beat.

Orion?

ORION. We got into a thing and they were spinning me some
bullshit about power dynamics but basically she doesn't
want to have intimate scenes with a Black guy.

LOIS. I definitely want to have intimate scenes with this Black
guy /

ORION. Why?

LOIS. Why you asking me that?

ORION. Anyway maybe I don't want to be kissing no White
woman either /

Beat.

LOIS. Well I'm going to run my man a bath.

Then serve him something nice after.

LOIS *exits*.

ORION *sees the laptop – grabs it and takes a seat –*
He opens it up –

VOICE (*the voice has a very weird hyper-fake*
Jamaican/American accent). So today we're making rice and
peas. It is not that much of a mystery you know. It's actually
easier than you think and there isn't a single Jamaican
grandma in sight!!

Laughter –

This dish originated from the Caribbean but is fast becoming
one of the staples of all our dinner tables…

Get ready to rock your Caribbean kitchen skills!

Loud fake-sounding Soca music plays –

ORION *is motionless –*

ORION. Fuck I'm tired!

BLACK NOVA *enters*.

BLACK NOVA. I know everything reminds you of her.
I know…

ORION *begins a ritualistic dance –*

Whew.
Chile.
This game.
This race.
What a time.

BLACK NOVA *breaks into song again. It is a song of*
protest. A cacophony of the noise of protest. Of gunshots.
Snatches of speeches. Protest songs. Children crying. 'I can't
breathe' chants over and over. The office banter. The minstrel
song. The stomping of feet. The cry for help, the endless
chatter, the National Anthem, the endless clapping.

ROO *enters*.

LOIS *enters*.

LOIS. What are you doing here?

ROO. Are you really asking me that?

LOIS. I just… you know… you moved out so /

ROO. And you moved in. So! My brother called me.

You moved right into what is not yours. But I don't blame you
you know. That's all you know. When was the last time you
asked anyone if it was right… alright… to just take something?

LOIS. He said it was cool for me to /

ROO. Only after you had made this space uninhabitable for me.
Only when you had interrupted what we had. Without even
thinking to ask. And look at my things.
Look at this violence Lois.
Can't you see it?
These aren't just things. They are the things I use to speak
with… to other *Black* women. And you've come with your
paws and dirtied them. Because why shouldn't you. Yeah.

LOIS. That's not it! I guess I was just trying to understand /

ROO. How about don't try.
How about don't guess.
How about accepting that some things don't live in you.
That no matter how much fake tan, how much you try and fit
into the same clothes, no matter you don't feel it. You're just
playing with something that is no game.

BLACK NOVA. But here we are…
Still here…

ORION (*to* LOIS). What do you see when you look at me?

LOIS. I see what you could be Orion without this burden.
I see potential /

ORION. There is no…
I'm not…

I'm whole. You see potential or something already whole?
All of me existing right now.
There's nothing for you to make better /

LOIS. We can all be better.

That's the game right?

ORION. But only some are allowed to be enough. Wholly.
Enough.

Right?

LOIS *moves towards him. Realises it's too late.* LOIS *exits.*

4. Home

ORION *sits.*

ROO *enters.*

Beat.

ORION. That dress…

ROO. It was just there you know in her things…

ORION. It suits you Roo.

Beat.

ROO. We can go see her any time you know…
Go talk to her.
She said she would always be…

ORION. Standing there.
It's still not the same.
That is not her down there!

This space…
This life she gave us…
What's left of what she is?
I keep looking and…

ROO. Do you think she's alright Or?
Do you think she knows how much we love her for loving us?

ORION. We can show her by loving ourselves just as hard.

ROO. Remember the way she used to cuss Dad out if he played a trick on her.
Oh my days remember when he put that big plastic snake just under one of the cushions. And she freaked out and screamed like she'd seen a ghost /

ORION. 'Let me tell you something right here and now you think what you doing is a joke. Yeah. You think you're funny. A real joker yeah. The joke is on you because your ankles ashy like used coal so you go laugh at someone else. And get out of my house. Go eat someone else food tonight.'

ROO. And then he would turn on the charm –

ORION. 'The way your lips curl up like that when you talk Cyn. It like God painted them lips himself.'

ROO. And her screw-face like –

'Well I pity you because this is the last time you gon ever have anything to do with these lips unless I'm telling this whole street what a good-for-nothing' /

ORION. And then he would walk over to the record player like this innit –

ORION *skanks across the room, miming the action of someone placing a needle on a record –*

ROO. Something real smooth yeah like Gregory Abbott…

ORION. Dancing –

And then he would do that dance towards her /

ROO. And you could see her just… just… and… and she would just…

ORION. We were her Aurora and Orion. And she was…

Black Love is the day my mother opened her Black legs and
let my Black father come inside her Black-framed
sacredness...
Black Love is my name
Black Love is the look from my Black grandmother that
burned itself through skin, soul and spirit
Black Love is that red dust I remember inhaling
Black Love is my mouth wide open waiting to be fed by Black
breasts
Black Love is watching my brothers and my sister be born
from that same Black place
Black Love is the sun on my face in a place where my
Blackness is not a question
Black Love is every day I look in the mirror and accept
myself
Black Love is my daughter's name
Black Love is everything I can do to not believe in your
version of me
Black Love is...
Black Love is...
Black Love is...
Black Love is...

ROO. And we're still here /

ORION. We will find new light for those that are gone!

- **Two Black people who share a very similar culture and history being able to come together to love each other unapologetically. Celebrating their Blackness and the power in that. A love that exalts Black women and respects them as the real head of the house...**

- **Black Love has to be unrelenting resilient in order to withstand any pitfalls that other relationship, without the need to survive, might succumb to in falling apart.**

- **Is finding the person who sees and loves me no matter what.**

- **Feels right. Less explaining. Less explaining away.**

- **When we love we don't just appreciate the beauty of our skin with its scars, we feel our ancestors, generations, years of whole histories colliding victoriously after being torn apart, beaten, scattered across the earth. But here we are, now, winning, with Black Love...**

BLACK NOVA. We are...

ROO *and* ORION. Joy Gardner. Simeon Francis. Kingsley Burrell. Smiley Culture. Roger Sylvester. Sarah Reed. Cherry Groce. Jimmy Mubenga. Dalian Atkinson. Cynthia Jarrett. Julian Cole. David Oluwale. Mark Duggan. Christopher Alder. Sean Rigg. Rashan Charles. Sheku Bayoh. Michael Powell. Leon Briggs. Ricky Bishop. Adrian Thompson. Aston McLean. Edson Da Costa. Olaseni Lewis. Nicole Smallman. Bibaa Henry. Richard Okorogheye.

Song: 'Bones Broken'

They don't want to hear.
So the chase, the game begins again.

The whole CAST *leave the stage –*

The names appear across the walls/screens –

BLACK NOVA*'s song changes during this speech. It is the sound of Black girls' skipping games. The sound of the water. Of birds. Words in Yoruba, the sound of a kora, the sound of prayers. Of carnival sound systems. Of endless blue skies. Of stars exploding. Of joy. Of joy. Of joy.*

The End.

A Nick Hern Book

Black Love first published in Great Britain in 2021 as a paperback original by Nick Hern Books Limited, The Glasshouse, 49a Goldhawk Road, London W12 8QP, in association with Paines Plough, Belgrade Theatre Coventry and tiata fahodzi

Black Love copyright © 2021 Chinonyerem Odimba

Chinonyerem Odimba has asserted her moral right to be identified as the author of this work

Cover photograph: Rebecca Nead-Menear; graphic design: Michael Windsor-Ungureanu

Designed and typeset by Nick Hern Books, London
Printed in the UK by Mimeo Ltd, Huntingdon, Cambridgeshire PE29 6XX

A CIP catalogue record for this book is available from the British Library

ISBN 978 1 83904 024 5